AF443987

Digital Marketing

Digital
marketing
Pro
Secrets

Learn Digital
Marketing Pro Secrets

Digital Marketing

Digital marketing Pro Secrets

AUTHOR NAME

Praveen Kumar

Copyright © All rights reserved worldwide.

YOUR RIGHTS: This book is restricted to your personal use only. It does not come with any other rights.

LEGAL DISCLAIMER: This book is protected by international copyright law and may not be copied, reproduced, given away, or used to create derivative works without the publisher's expressed permission. The publisher retains full copyrights to this book.

The author has made every reasonable effort to be as accurate and complete as possible in the creation of this book and to ensure that the information provided is free from errors; however, the author/publisher/ reseller assumes no responsibility for errors, omissions, or contrary interpretation of the subject matter herein and does not warrant or represent at

Any time that the contents within are accurate due to the rapidly changing nature of the Internet.

Any perceived slights of specific persons, peoples, or organizations are unintentional.

The purpose of this book is to educate and there are no guarantees of income, sales or results implied. The publisher/author/reseller can therefore not be held accountable for any poor results you may attain when implementing the techniques or when following any guidelines set out for you in this book.

Any product, website, and company names mentioned in this report are the trademarks or copyright properties of their respective owners. The author/publisher/reseller are not associated or affiliated with them in any way. Nor does the referred product, website, and company names sponsor, endorse, or approve this product.

COMPENSATION DISCLOSURE: Unless otherwise expressly stated, you should assume that the links contained in this book may be affiliate links and either the author/publisher/reseller will earn commission if you click on them and buy the product/service mentioned in this book. However, the author/publisher/reseller disclaims any liability that may result from your involvement with any such websites/products. You should perform due diligence before buying

Mentioned products or services.

This constitutes the entire license
agreement. Any disputes or terms
not discussed in this agreement are
at the sole discretion of the
publisher.

Table of Contents

Introduction

Dear reader this book contain full of Digital marketers Pro Secrets. This Book helps you to become a successful digital marketer. In this Digital marketing book I will help you to guide you step by step process in order to become a successful in online Business. No matter If you are a beginner to Digital marketing field.

I will help you to provide the ultimate secret guide to become a Successful entrepreneur. Now day's technology is growing day by day many new Innovations growing day by day. In order to become a successful in online business you should update your skills daily.

Before Investing on Business you must invest yourself by developing your skills every day.

Before Providing Digital marketing pro secrets you must know basic of Digital marketing. Here I am going to reveal all the secrets of Digital marketing From Base to Pro. Let's Dive in to Digital marketing.

What is Digital Marketing?

Digital Marketing is the term used for marketing of products or services using digital technologies to reach the viewers, turn them into customers, and retain them.

How digital marketing differ from old Method marketing?

The Old manner of marketing involved businesses to advertise their products or services on print media, radio and television commercials, business cards, bill boards, and in many other similar ways where Internet or social media websites were not employed for advertising. Old method marketing policies had limited customer reachability and scope of driving customers' buying behavior.

Digital marketing achieves targets of marketing a business through different online channels. Let us see how.

The following lists a few points that explains digital marketing from old marketing

About Old Marketing:

1. Communication is unidirectional. Means, a business communicates about its products or services with a group of people.

2. Medium of communication is generally phone calls, letters, and Emails.

3. Campaigning takes more time for designing, preparing, and launching.

4. It is carried out for a specific audience throughout from generating campaign ideas up to selling a product or a service.

5. It is conventional way of marketing; best for reaching local audience.

6. It is difficult to measure the effectiveness of a

campaign.

About Digital Marketing

1. Communication is bidirectional. The customer also can ask queries or make suggestions about the business products and services.

2. Medium of communication is mostly through social media websites, chat, and Email.

3. There is always a fast way to develop an online campaign and carry out changes along its development. With digital tools, campaigning is easier.

4. The content is available for general public. It is then made to reach the specific audience by employing search engine techniques.

5. It is best for reaching global audience.

6. It is easier to measure the effectiveness of a campaign through analytics.

Types of Digital marketing

Search Engine Optimization (SEO)

Blogging

Search Engine Marketing

Social Media Marketing

Content Marketing

Affiliate Marketing

Influencer Marketing

Email Marketing

Viral Marketing

Advertising

Search Engine Optimization (SEO)

Search engine optimization (SEO) is the process of increasing the quality and quantity of website traffic by increasing the visibility of a website or a web page to users of a web search engine.

SEO refers to the improvement of unpaid results known as organic" results and excludes direct traffic/visitors and the purchase of paid placement.

SEO may target different kinds of searches, including image search, video search, academic search,news search, and industry-specific vertical search engines.

Optimizing a website may involve editing its content, adding content, and modifying HTML and associated coding to both increase its relevance to specific keywords and remove barriers to the indexing activities of search engines like Google ,Yahoo etc.Promoting a site to increase the number of backlinks, or inbound links, is another SEO tactic.

As an Digital marketing strategy, SEO considers how search engines work, the computer-programmed algorithms that dictate search engine behavior, what people search for, the actual search terms or keywords typed into search engines, and which search engines are preferred by their targeted audience. SEO is performed because a website will receive more visitors from a search engine the higher the website ranks in the search engine results page (SERP). These visitors can then be converted into customers.

SEO differs from local search engine optimization in that the latter is focused on optimizing a business' online presence so that its web pages will be displayed by search engines when a user enters a local search for its products or services. The former instead is more focused on national or international searches.

Blogging

A blogging (shorten of "weblog") is an online journal or informational website displaying information in the reverse chronological order, with the latest posts appearing first. It is a platform where a writer or even a group of writers share their views on an individual subject.

Uses of Blogging

There are many reasons to start a blogging for personal use and only a handful of strong ones for business blogging. Blogging for business, projects, or anything else that might bring you money has a very straightforward purpose – to rank your website higher in Google SERPs, a.k.a. increase your visibility.

As a business, you rely on consumers to keep buying your products and services. As a new business, you rely on blogging to help you get to these consumers and grab their attention. Without blogging, your website would remain invisible, whereas running a blog makes you searchable and competitive.

So, the main purpose of a blog is to connect you to the relevant audience. Another one is to boost your traffic and send quality leads to your website.

The more frequent and better your blog posts are, the higher the chances for your website to get discovered and visited by your target audience. Which means, a blog is an effective lead generation tool. Add a great call to action (CTA), and it will convert your website traffic into high-quality leads. But a blog also allows you to showcase your authority and build a brand.

When you use your niche knowledge for creating informative and engaging posts, it builds trust with your audience. Great blogging makes your business looks more credible, which is especially important if your brand is still young and fairly unknown. It ensures presence and authority at the same time.

In the early 2000s, blogging emerged in all different phases when several political blogs were born. Also, blogs with how-to manuals began to appear. Established institutions began to note the difference between journalism and blogging. The number of bloggers in the United States is set to reach 31.7 million users in 2020.

Definition of blogging

Blogging is the set of many skills that one needs to run and control a blog. Equipping web page with tools to make the process of writing, posting, linking, and sharing content easier on the internet.

Why is blogging so popular?

It's important to mention that blogging grows with each passing day! Hence, to answer the question 'what is blogging' we need to look at the factors behind its rise.

In the early stages, blogs became mainstream, as news services began using them as tools for outreach and opinion forming. It became a new source of information.Through Blogging

Companies keeps clients and customers upto date. Through a blog visitors can comment and interact with you or your brand. You can also earn money through blogging.

To know how to setup blogging please check one of my book name called blogging setup on Amazon.

Search Engine Marketing

Search engine marketing (SEM) is a form of Internet marketing that involves the promotion of websites by increasing their visibility in search engine results pages (SERPs) primarily through paid advertising.SEM may incorporate search engine optimization (SEO), which adjusts or rewrites website content and site architecture to achieve a higher ranking in search engine results pages to enhance pay per click (PPC) listings

Search engine marketing is the practice of marketing a business using paid advertisements that appear on search engine results pages (or SERPs). Advertisers bid on keywords that users of services such as Google and Bing might enter when looking for certain products or services, which gives the advertiser the opportunity for their ads to appear alongside results for those search queries.

These ads, often known by the term pay-per-click ads, come in a variety of formats. Some are small, text-based ads, whereas others, such as product listing ads (PLAs, also known as Shopping ads) are more visual, product-based advertisements that allow consumers to see important information at-a-glance, such as price and reviews.

Search engine marketing's greatest strength is that it offers advertisers the opportunity to put their ads in front of motivated customers who are ready to buy at the precise moment they're ready to make a purchase. No other advertising medium can do this, which is why search engine marketing is so effective and such an amazingly powerful way to grow your business.

Search engine optimization VS Search Engine Marketing

Generally, "search engine marketing" refers to paid search marketing, a system where businesses pay Google to show their ads in the search results.

Search engine optimization, or SEO, is different because businesses don't pay Google for traffic and clicks; rather, they earn a free spot in in the search results by having the most relevant content for a given keyword search.

Both SEO and SEM should be fundamental parts of your online marketing strategy. SEO is a powerful way to drive evergreen traffic at the top of the funnel, while search engine advertisements are a highly cost-effective way to drive conversions at the bottom of the funnel.

Social Media Marketing

Social Media Marketing is the manner of generating website traffic or attracting viewers and customers through social networking websites such as Facebook, Instagram, Pinterest, LinkedIn, Twitter, and so on. Social media marketing is a subset of digital marketing.

All social networking websites support sharing of content, but all are not necessarily employed for digital marketing. While Facebook emphasizes on personal sharing, Twitter emphasizes on tweeting short messages about ones' opinions or reactions, and LinkedIn goes for professional networking, Pinterest motivates to market one's ideas and online businesses.

Principle of Social Media Marketing

Social media grew up as the most popular outcome of the Internet as people around the world like to communicate and share their special moments, problems, ideas, and suggestions with others. They also like to learn about a place worth visiting, a new craft projects, recipes, or a new language. Social media websites enable you to share content of your choice with right audience at your convenience.

This popularity of social media has inspired the business minds around the world with the idea of small online businesses. One can open a store in Amazon, eBay, or Create any other custom platforms by your self-using web design and if are a beginner don't worry hire professional web designer at decent cost. I am a Chief executive officer at loyalwebsite.com I am offering free web design we charge only for hosting service for more detail you can check our website. Now days building an online store are very easy. But the main challenge is finding the customers. There are ways like search results in Google, Bing or in any other search engine. But for a new business with established competitors, it takes a long time to get a high rank in the search results.

Social networking websites are a great solution to this challenge. The basic technique here is to share engaging posts and the right content created for the desired audience. Then the audience helps by sharing the content further, which in turn reaches further. Hence there is another option of advertising the product, services, or ideas on the social networking websites where there is less degree of competition.

Content marketing

Content marketing is a strategic marketing approach focused on creating and distributing valuable, relevant, and consistent content to attract and retain a clearly defined audience — and, ultimately, to drive profitable customer action.

Content marketing is a form of marketing focused on creating, publishing, and distributing content for a targeted audience online. It is often used by businesses in order to:

- Attract attention and generate leads
- Expand their customer base
- Generate or increase online sales
- Increase brand awareness or credibility

Engage an online community of users

Content marketing attracts prospects and transforms prospects into customers by creating and sharing valuable free content. Content marketing helps companies create sustainable brand loyalty, provides valuable information to consumers, and creates a willingness to purchase products from the company in the future. This relatively new form of marketing does not involve direct sales. Instead, it builds trust and rapport with the audience.

Unlike other forms of online marketing, content marketing relies on anticipating and meeting an existing customer need for information, as opposed to creating demand for a new need. As James O'Brien of Contently wrote on Mash able, "The idea central to content marketing is that a brand must give something valuable to get something valuable in return. Instead of the commercial, be the show. Instead of the banner ad, be the feature story. Content marketing requires continuous delivery of large amounts of content, preferably within a content marketing strategy.

When businesses pursue content marketing, the main focus should be the needs of the prospect or customer. Once a business has identified the customer's need, information can be presented in a variety of formats, including news, video, white papers, e-books, info graphics, email newsletters, case studies, podcasts, how-to guides, question and answer articles, photos, blogs, etc. Most of these formats belong to the digital channels.

Affiliate marketing

Affiliate marketing is the process by which an affiliate earns a commission for marketing another person's or company's products. The affiliate simply searches for a product they enjoy, then promotes that product and earns a piece of the profit from each sale they make. The sales are tracked via affiliate links from one website to another.

How Affiliate Marketing Works?

Affiliate marketing works by spreading the responsibilities of product marketing and creation across parties; it manages to leverage the abilities of a variety of individuals for a more effective marketing strategy while providing contributors with a share of the profit. To make this work, three different parties must be involved:

Let's delve into the complex relationship these three parties share to ensure affiliate marketing is a success.

Seller or product producers

The seller or whether a solo entrepreneur or large

enterprise is a vendor, merchant, product creator, retailer with a product to market. The product can be a physical object, like household goods, or a service, like makeup tutorials. Also known as the brand, the seller does not need to be actively involved in the marketing, but they may also be the advertiser and profit from the revenue sharing associated with affiliate marketing.

The affiliates or advertiser

Also known as a publisher, the affiliate can be either an individual or a company that markets the seller's product in an appealing way to potential consumers. In other words, the affiliate promotes the product to persuade consumers that it is valuable or beneficial to them and convince them to purchase the product. If the consumer does end up buying the product, the affiliate receives a portion of the revenue made.

Affiliates often have a very specific audience, to whom they market, generally adhering to that audience's interests. This creates a defined niche or personal brand that helps the affiliate attract consumers who will be most likely to act on the promotion.

The consumer

Whether the consumer knows it or not, they (and their purchases) are the drivers of affiliate marketing. Affiliates share these products with them on social media, blogs, and websites.

When consumers buy the product, the seller and the affiliate share the profits. Sometimes the affiliate will choose to be upfront with the consumer by disclosing that they are receiving commission for the sales they make. Other times the consumer may be completely oblivious to the affiliate marketing infrastructure behind their purchase.

Either way, they will rarely pay more for the product purchased through affiliate marketing; the affiliate's share of the profit is included in the retail price. The consumer will complete the purchase process and receive the product as normal, unaffected by the affiliate marketing system in which they are a significant part.

In order to grow your business 100 times faster you should have affiliate marketing program on your business. This will help you to grow your because ultimate speed by of paying some commissions to your Affiliate's.

Influencer marketing

Influencer marketing is a form of social media marketing involving endorsements and product placement from influencers, people and organizations that have a purported expert level of knowledge or social influence in their field. Influencer content may be framed as testimonial advertising; influencers play the role of a potential buyer, or may be involved as third parties. These third parties can be seen in the supply chain (such as retailers or manufacturers) or as value-added influencers, such as journalists, academics, industry analysts, and professional advisers.

How to choose Influencers?

The best way to choose influencer's is through Social media, here are my some of best recommended social media platforms are Youtube and Instagram.

Many Influencers' are getting high free 1 million traffics every day all you need to do is contact the influencer's and pay some money.

After paid ask them to post your business website links on their profile and their feature post. Before paying them money you must choose the best influencers according to your business niche.

For example: If your business is any kind of fitness related products then go to YouTube and search fitness related niche . Now you need to select top 10 videos on result and check the description whether they are selling any products or they trying to promote any other products .If they not promote any products then ask them to promote your products for one month or one week and check the result for one week if you get any sale keep them, and if you not get any sale then cancel their relationship and search for other influencer's according to your niche.

Email Marketing

Email marketing is the act of sending a commercial message, typically to a group of people, using email. In its broadest sense, every email sent to a potential or current customer could be considered email marketing. It usually involves using email to send advertisements, request business, or solicit sales or donations, and is meant to build loyalty, trust, or brand awareness. Marketing emails can be sent to a purchased lead list or a current customer database. The term usually refers to sending email messages with the purpose of enhancing a merchant's relationship with current or previous customers, encouraging customer loyalty and repeat business, acquiring new customers or convincing current customers to purchase something immediately, and sharing third-party ads.

Email marketing is the highly effective in digital marketing of sending emails to prospects and customers. Effective marketing emails convert prospects into customers, and turn one-time buyers into loyal, raving fans.

Do you known Email is the No: 1 communication channel and at least 99% of consumers check their email on a daily basis? That can't be said of any other communication channel.

If You are own your email list. On any social media platform, your account along with all your fans and posts could be suspended or deleted at any time, for any reason, without notice. However, you own your email list. No one can take those leads away from you.

Email just converts better. People who buy products marketed through email spend 138% more than those who do not receive email offers. In fact, email marketing has an ROI of 4400%. That's huge! And if you are wondering if social media converts even better, think again: the average order value of an email is at least three times higher than that of social media.

Build an Email List

Wondering how to build email list? Email marketing is made up of several moving pieces, but that doesn't mean it has to be complicated.

Here's how it breaks down...

How to collect your email list? There are many companies are available to provide email services they will charge according to your email asset monthly basic.

Up to 2000 emails some few companies are offering free email service such as mailchimp, constant contact etc.

Email service provider has made it super easy to start collecting leads right away, even without an email marketing service, with Leads integration.

With Leads, you can begin building your email list, and even begin reaching out to leads, while keeping your leads stored safely inside your email service provider dashboard. Then, when you're ready...

You add an email service provider. There are a ton of them out there, but we take the guesswork out and make it really easy to choose the right one for you and your goals.

After those two steps, it's just a matter refining your lists and your messaging so you're reaching your audience and really connecting with them. Plus, you'll be able to set up some automation in your email service which will make things much easier for you.

How to Grow your Email List?

What most people do when they want to build an email list is to put an option form on their website and hope that people sign up. Unfortunately, this strategy usually doesn't work very well.

To grow your email list, you need to attract people with a compelling offer. You need a lead magnet.

What is a Lead Magnet?

A lead magnet is something awesome that you give away for free in exchange for an email address. It doesn't have to cost you anything to create; most lead magnets are digital materials like PDFs, MP3 audio files, or videos that you can create yourself at minimal or no cost.

It can be absolutely anything you want, so long as it provides value to your visitors for free.

Sending email newsletters

More than 93% of business-to-business (B2B) marketers send email newsletters as part of their content marketing strategy. Email marketing is a very cost-effective way for brands to communicate with their customers and email newsletters are an essential piece of any email marketing strategy.

Viral marketing

Viral marketing or also called as viral advertising It is a business strategy that uses existing social networks to promote a product. Its name refers to how consumers spread information about a product with other people, much in the same way that a virus spreads from one person to another. It can be delivered by word of mouth or enhanced by the network effects of the Internet and mobile networks.

Viral Marketing is that which is able to generate interest and the potential sale of a brand or product through messages that spread like a virus, in other words, quickly, and from person to person. The idea is for it to be the users themselves that choose to share the content.

Due to their speed and ease to share, social networks are the natural habitat of this kind of marketing. The most widespread example in recent times is the creation of moving, surprising or spectacular videos on YouTube, which are then shared on Facebook, Twitter and other channels.

The reason to make use or viral, the ease in spreading and sharing, is however a double-edged sword. We cannot forget that in this type of campaign, a large part of the control falls into the hands of the users, and we risk the message being misinterpreted or parodied. On the other hand, a successful viral campaign can work miracles for your brand's results.

How viral Marketing works?

A viral marketing campaign is very simple to carry out: create a video or another type of content which is attractive to the target put it on the internet and plans the first actions to get it moving. From there on, all you can do is wait for the fuse to light and for users to start sharing like crazy.

In some cases, viral happens by accident, from a video uploaded by a private user that all of a sudden becomes popular and begins to circulate all around the Internet.

As for the dispersion strategy of the videos

created by brands, we have two focus points: the shown or the concealed. In the former, the user is aware from the first moment that they are viewing advertising content, while in the latter the participation of the brand is hidden and is only revealed later.

If you apply concealed marketing techniques, it is important to be very careful so the user does not feel tricked, cheated or deceived, as the viral campaign could then turn against you.

No matter what strategy we choose, we should never ever become spammers, nor go overboard while sharing the content. Instead of repeating message over and over again, the best strategy is to find the perfect place and time and let the "viral fuse" light itself.

Advertising

Advertising is a marketing tactic involving paying for space to promote a product, service, or cause. The actual promotional messages are called advertisements, or ads for short. The goal of advertising is to reach people most likely to be willing to pay for a company's products or services and entice them to buy.

Advertising provides a direct line of communication to your existing and prospective customers about your product or service.

Your advertising goals should be established in your business plan. For example, you may want to obtain a certain percentage of growth in sales, generate more inquiries for sales, or build in-store traffic. The desired result can simply be increasing name recognition or modifying the image you're projecting. Objectives vary depending on the industry and market you're in.

All products and businesses go through three stages, with different advertising goals for each one.

For start-up business: You're new in the market and need to establish your identity. Your company needs high levels of promotion and publicity to grab consumers' attention.

For Growing business: Once your identity is established, you need to differentiate yourself from your competition and convince buyers that yours is the service or product to try.

For established business: The purpose at this point is to remind consumers why they should continue buying from you.

No matter which stage your business is in, advertising follows four steps, according to the industry mnemonic, "AIDA: Awareness, Interest, Desire, Action." Your job is to make prospective customers aware that your product or service exists, pique their interest in what your product or service can do for them, make them want to try your product or service, and finally take action, by asking for more information or actually buying the product.

When developing an advertising campaign, complete the following four-step procedure:

How to define your market: Determine who your target market is (those customers most likely to buy your product or service). One magazine that fun to read, interesting and helpful in this regard is American Demographics.

How to establish your budget: You know what you can afford to spend to reach your target audience.

How to Plan which media you to use: Figure out what are the best ways to reach your prospective customers with your message.

Create an advertising strategy: Choose the most effective message and visuals for your advertising campaign.

Advantage of Advertising

Advertising Makes customers aware of your product or service,

It helps to convince customers that your company's product or service is right for their needs;

You can easily target the desire person for your product or service;

It helps to enhance the image of your company;

It helps to promote your new products or services worldwide at very fast.

Traffic sources

Traffic is the flow of internet users on the internet. When it comes to affiliate marketing, you need traffic directed to your offers or promotions in order to turn them into conversions.

There two types of traffic source they are

Free Traffic source

Paid Traffic source

Free Traffic Source

In order to get free traffic source all you need to do is work daily by posting content every day to get free traffic source for your business

Types of free Traffic source

Search Engine Optimization

Search Engine Optimization is the process of improving a website's visibility in a search engine's search results. Typically, the higher up the rankings a website is shown on a search engine, the more traffic it will receive. This is called, natural traffic as you aren't directly paying the search engine to show your website in its results. SEO isn't limited to text search.

Social Media Marketing

Social Marketing is a form of internet marketing on any social media platform or website. Social media means any platform that indulges a group of internet-based applications and audience to exchange content. The majority of social media platforms can operate on any platform or device. Youtube Facebook Instagram and Twitter are two of the biggest examples.

Paid Traffic source

 Paid traffic source is the best method to generate lead fast and easy. For paid source required only money and small skills to build a successful campaign.

Pay Per Click

Pay-Per-Click is an internet advertising model used to drive traffic to websites. The advertiser typically pays a fixed charge for every click that is sent to their website. They generally set a bid on relative keywords that are searched via PPC search engines. The advertiser with the highest bid is then placed in the highest position on the rankings

Cost per impression

Cost per impression (CPI) refers to the rate that an advertiser has agreed to pay per 1,000 views of a particular advertisement. A website that serves ads based on CPI doesn't need the user to click on the ad — each appearance of the ad in front of a user counts as one impression

Conversion Ads

An action that's counted when someone interacts with your ad (for example, clicks a text ad or views a video ad) and then takes an action that you've defined as valuable to your business, such as an online purchase or a call to your business from a mobile phone.

Why conversion ads

See which keywords, ads, ad groups, and campaigns are best at driving valuable customer activity.

Understand your return on investment (ROI) and make better informed decisions about your ad spend.

Use Smart Bidding strategies (such as Maximize Conversions, target CPA, and target ROAS) that automatically optimize your campaigns according to your business goals.

See how many customers may be interacting with your ads on one device or browser and converting on another. You can view cross-device, cross-browser, and other conversion data in your "All conversions" reporting column.

About Engagement ads

The total numbers of actions that people take involving your adverts

Engagement ads run on the Google Display Network (GDN) and use the same flexible targeting options as normal display campaigns. Google has also announced additional self-service ad formats, including Cross Device ads, a YouTube Masthead Lightbox to aid in consistent branding across ad formats, and a Shopping Catalog Lightbox, which allows users to display multiple products from a merchant center account.

These campaigns are only available on a cost-per-engagement basis, which allows advertisers to bid and pay only if a user has engaged with their ads defines "engagement" as a user moussing over the ad for more than two seconds. This delay eliminates accidental interactions which could be charged on this pricing model.

Engagement indicates that your ads are relevant to your target audience, which helps your ads perform better. When people see ads that are relevant to them, they're more likely to interact with those ads. This metric lets you measure these interactions and compare them to engagement from other ads or campaigns.

Engagement includes all actions that people take involving your ads while they're running. Post engagements can include actions such as reacting to, commenting on or sharing the ad, claiming an offer, viewing a photo or video, or clicking on a link.

Steps to promote your products & Services

It's time to start driving traffic to your store and close your sales. Whether you're trying to make your first sale or you've been open for business for a while, it's always good to find more ways to promote your products.

You could be offering the best new product or service in the world, but if you don't promote it properly, you may end up losing money down the line. Here are some creative ways to promote a new service or product for your small business.

How to Promote your Products or Services?

When it comes to promoting a new product or service for your business, it can seem like there are endless options. It can be difficult to figure out where to get started and which methods of promotion will give you the best results. The truth is that there are many ways to promote your business, and what works may depend on your business. Here are some Best step by step ways to promote service or product for your business.

Offers an Exclusive Preview or Trails to Customers

Your customers are a key part of how to promote your products or services, because they are most likely the first ones who will buy it. Offer customers an exclusive preview or trail of your new products or services. This can take the form of a private, pre-launch party, an online preview, or a special invitation to test out your latest service. These exclusive offers to your customers will make them feel good and keep them coming back.

Steps for free Traffic source

Submit your website in all top search engines such as Google, Bing, Duckduckgo ect. You can submit in Google search engine by using Google search console, for Bing use Bing webmaster tool. This will help you to get free traffics daily from all over the world. Search engines help us to connect people worldwide.

Steps to promote on Social Media

Nowadays people are very interested to connect with social media because everything is there in social media. Join some of my recommended top social Medias such as Facebook, Instagram, Twitter, Tik tok, Reddit, Pinterest ect.

For products or services please create a new professional page don't use your personal account. But you must share your page link on your personal account because it helps to connect your friends and family with your business.

Connect with groups particularly on Facebook groups and post your products or service on the group will get more engagement on your post this will lead to more free traffics to your website.

To get more followers and likes on your page you must engage with social media daily and you need to give likes and comments on others recent post. This makes others to engage with your page and they will visit your page and they follow you most.

Social Media Offers

Offers and giveaways are a very popular tool among top quality marketers. Why? Marketers know that social media contests work!

Social media offers are a fun, easy way of connecting with customers and bringing in more fans for your social media platforms. A simple Facebook contest for example, garners 34% new fans on average per campaign. That's huge considering that organic reach is low on

Facebook!

Instagram giveaways give customers an exclusive chance to be the first person to get their hands on your new product—for free! The giveaway can be marketed all across your social media channels and through email. Run an Instagram giveaway to get more direct traffic, put your business in front of new customers, and for a fun way to connect with fans.

You can giveaways Related eBooks, products or services, or any kind of free tech related products this will boost your page and you will get more leads that you can convert them into your customers.

Steps to Promote Email Marketing

Collecting customer's emails is the best asset which converts into lifelong income. Email is one of the most consistently effective channels for acquiring new customers. And while channels like search can take a while to start generating organic traffic, email marketing can start working right away. That's why you should be using email to promote your store.

There's no need to spend all your time writing and sending emails. Make it easy on yourself by setting up a collection of automated email campaigns that are designed to increase your revenue. There are many options available, such as:

1. Emailing new subscribers and offering them an incentive to shop this will increase your sale and traffics every day.

2. Emailing new customers will chance to increase the sales.

3. Emailing the visitors via Notification email who abandoned their cart and reminding them to finish their purchase this will also increase and sales.

Steps for Advertising

If you have money and don't have time to spend with your business or social media then advertising is the best way to promote your products and services, advertising are the best way to get professional valid customers to have an idea or interested to buy your products or services.

The best advertising companies are Google ads, Facebook ads and Bing ads are my best recommended advertising companies were you will get best traffics that can be easily converted to customers.

Conclusion

Hi readers finally from my experience Digital marketing is the best way to promote your products and service around the worldwide, If you are not in Digital marketing field then you will be lose. If you want to be a **SUCEFULL BUSINESSMAN** in the world then you must know Digital marketing, Digital marketing is peace of Art you should know all Types of Digital marketing, If you want more free traffics to your website you should have Professional Social media page in all top social media accounts. You must create content daily and you need to post your content daily in order to get more customers.

If you are a lazy person and don't have time to post on social media then don't worry you can go with Advertising but you need money. Please spend at least minimum 10$ per day for per ad set. For 10$ you will get minimum 10 leads to 15 leads per day. According to your niche you should calculate the percentage of sales. Don't think if you spend money you will get customers and they will buy your products. You need to create a trust this will take some time. To get some 3 to 5 sales per day you need to drive traffics at least 50 to 100 leads per day to your website. This will happen fast if you spend money. If you don't have money to promote your website then sales will grow slowly.

Products don't sell themselves; fortunately, there are many ways to promote your products and services. I gave many methods to promote your products or services. According to your confortable you can find the steps from the list above and follow the step by step guide to learn how to do it!

www.ingramcontent.com/pod-product-compliance
Lightning Source LLC
Chambersburg PA
CBHW030403160726
47992CB00007B/2946